UPDATED EDITION

# Love Letters from God

## Bible Stories for a Girl's Heart

*Written by*
## Glenys Nellist
*Illustrated by*
## Rachel Clowes

ZONDERkidz

*This book is dedicated to my sisters:*
*Pam, Pauline, and Angela—*
*The Encouraging Girls. I love you.*
*—G.N.*

*To Ben, Samuel, Patrick and Harry with love.*
*—R.C.*

ZONDERKIDZ

*Love Letters from God: Bible Stories for a Girl's Heart*
Copyright © 2017 by Glenys Nellist
Illustrations © 2017 by Rachel Clowes

This title is also available as a Zondervan ebook. Visit www.zondervan.com/ebooks.

Requests for information should be addressed to:

Zonderkidz, 3900 *Sparks Dr. SE, Grand Rapids, Michigan* 49546

Hardcover ISBN 978-0-310-15474-7
epub ISBN 978-0-310-75309-4

*Art direction and design: Jody Langley*

*Printed in India*

23 24 25 26 27 28 /REP/ 22 21 20 19 18 17 16 15 14 13 12 11 10 9 8 7 6 5 4 3 2 1

# Stories

# The First Girl

*Genesis 3*

God beamed in delight as Eve opened her eyes for the very first time. She was wonderful! After six days of creating the world—painting the skies, stirring the seas, and filling the earth with life— here was God's masterpiece, a glorious finishing touch to the world. Here was Eve, made by God's own hand. And she was good.

God watched as Eve rose to her feet, grabbed Adam's hand, and ran barefoot through the garden. But someone else was watching Eve too. He was hiding quietly in the grass, watching and waiting for his chance to steal Eve's happiness. And one day, he made his move.

"Good morning, Eve," the slimy serpent whispered. "I'm going to try this delicious fruit for breakfast. Would you like some?"

"No," replied Eve. "I'm hungry, but that's the one fruit God told us not to eat. I can't stay in the garden if I eat that."

"Oh my goodness!" The serpent laughed. "You don't have to eat the whole thing! Surely God won't mind if you just try it?"

Eve took the fruit. She had never held, smelled, or seen a more delicious fruit. She took a bite and then gave some to Adam. In that instant, Eve knew she had done something terribly wrong. Now she would have to leave the Garden of Eden forever.

But before she left, God had a surprise for her. God was waiting at the gates to cover her with new, warm clothes. And as Eve walked away, she knew she was forever covered in God's love and forgiveness. God had made her, and she was good.

Dear _____,

Can you imagine how thrilled I was when I saw Eve? She was the very first girl I made, and she made creation complete. Did you know I feel the same way when I see you? Just like I made Eve, I made *you* too—and everything I make is good. So remember this—even if you make some bad choices, like Eve did, talk to me about it. I will cover you with my love and forgiveness, just like I covered Eve. You are good.

I Love You,

Your Creator,

GOD

5

# The Trusting Girl

*Exodus 2:1–10*

Miriam was hiding. As quiet as a mouse, she crouched, peeping through the tall reeds that grew on the bank of the Nile River. Miriam kept her eyes fixed on the little basket that was bobbing up and down at the water's edge. She was scared ... because in that little basket, down in the water, her baby brother lay fast asleep.

Miriam knew the river was the best place to hide him from the wicked king who wanted to hurt all the baby boys, but she was still scared. What if something terrible happened? Suppose the little basket sank? No—Miriam's mom made that basket super strong. It would not sink. Suppose the waves splashed over the edge of the little basket? No—the water was calm today. Miriam squeezed her eyes shut tight and tried to remember what her mom had told her. "Miriam," her mom had said. "We have to let go of all the things we're scared of. We have to trust that God will take care of our baby."

But it was hard to let go. Could Miriam do that?

Suddenly Miriam heard voices. She crouched down lower in the reeds and saw the king's daughter walking by the river. Oh no! What if she wanted to harm all the baby boys too? But guess what? The king's daughter loved babies! She scooped that little baby up out of the basket and cuddled him. "I will take care of you," she said. "But who will help me?"

"My mom will, my mom will!" shouted Miriam, as she ran out from her hiding place. And that is exactly what happened. Miriam laughed as she ran to tell her mom they could help take care of their own little boy! And as she ran, she thought about all the things she had been afraid of at the riverbank. The wicked king had not come. The waves had not come. But God had come. God had come and saved her baby brother. "Thank you, God," Miriam whispered, "for helping me let go of my fears and trust you instead."

Dear _____,

Do you ever get scared of things that *might* happen, like Miriam did? I want you to think about something that scares you. Now hold out your hand, put that scary thought right in the middle, and close your fingers tight around it. Now, slowly open your hand and just let that scary thought go. Let it fly far, far away into the air. Imagine instead that my great big, strong hand is holding on to your little one. Trust me. Let go of your fears and trust me.

Love,

GOD

# Rahab

# The Brave Girl

*Joshua 2*

Rahab knew trouble was coming. She peered out from her window and scanned the horizon to see if she could see the Israelite army. Everyone knew God's people would soon march into Jericho, and no one could stop them. The God of the Israelites was strong and powerful and mighty. Everyone heard the rumors of how this God made a path through the Red Sea so the Israelites could escape from Egypt. Rahab wanted to know a God like that. If their God could take care of those people in such a wonderful way, maybe God would take care of her too. Rahab was ready for a new start. She had made some bad choices. Was it too late for her to change, or could this God save her?

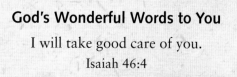

**God's Wonderful Words to You**

I will take good care of you.

Isaiah 46:4

8

Rahab caught a glimpse of two men running over the hills toward her house. Israelite spies! They had been sent to see what Jericho was like. Suddenly, Rahab knew what she had to do. She would welcome those spies and hide them in her home, even if it meant risking her life.

"Keep quiet. Don't say a word," Rahab whispered as she hid the two spies on her roof. "If the king finds you here, we will all be killed. When his men have gone, run to the hills. But when you return to Jericho with your army, please remember how I helped you. Please save me and my family. I want to follow your God who is the Maker of heaven and earth."

"We will," the men replied, as they scrambled down the scarlet rope that Rahab hung from her window. "Leave this red cord in place. It will be a sign to us that everyone in this house should be saved."

A few days later, the Israelite army marched into Jericho, and the walls of the city came crashing down. But brave Rahab and all the people who lived in the little house were saved. Rahab ran from Jericho, left her old life behind, and ran toward God. Her new life was waiting.

Dear _____,

Do you want to know what happened to Rahab after she left Jericho? Something wonderful! Rahab got married and had children. Those children had children—until one day, a *king* was born into Rahab's family. His name was King David. But Rahab's story doesn't end there. Many years later, from King David's family, another King was born—the King of the whole world, Jesus! How amazing that Jesus would come from Rahab's own family! I took good care of Rahab, and you can be sure I'll take good care of YOU too.

Your Caring Friend,
GOD

**God's Wonderful Words
to You**

You will receive the
strength you need when you
stay calm and trust in me.
Isaiah 30:15

Deborah

# The Strong Girl

*Judges 4 & 5*

Deborah sat quietly under the big palm tree, fanning herself with a leaf in the heat of the noonday sun. She was listening to God.

Deborah knew that her people, the Israelites, were in danger. She knew all about the wicked Sisera who had been cruel to the Israelites for twenty years. She knew how strong his army was. But Deborah also knew God was stronger. And calmly and confidently she sent for Barak, the leader of her army.

"Barak," she said. "Gather ten thousand men. God is going to help you defeat Sisera."

Dear _____,

Don't you wish you could have seen Deborah marching with those ten thousand men? What a wonderful sight to see! Do you know where Deborah's strength came from? It was me.

Deborah spent time with me every day, and she knew that I would help her be calm and strong when she needed it most.

Be calm. Be confident. Be strong. Trust in me.

Your Strong Friend,

GOD

"What?" Barak cried, as his knees started to knock. "Judge Deborah, did you know that Sisera has nine hundred chariots made of *iron*? I'm not going unless you come with me."

Deborah stood up and smiled. "Stay calm, Barak," she said quietly. "I will go with you."

Barak assembled his army and began to march toward Mount Tabor. His knees were still knocking, but Deborah's weren't. Calmly and confidently she marched alongside ten thousand men until they reached the mountain. "Go, Barak," she ordered. "God has gone ahead of you!" And it was true. As Barak marched out with his army, God overturned all those strong, iron chariots, and the Israelites won. Barak was overjoyed! Judge Deborah had so much to teach him about staying calm and trusting in God.

That evening, as the sun went down, Deborah and Barak sat together under the palm tree and sang a song of praise to God. And for the first time that day, Barak's knees stopped knocking.

# The Hopeful Girl

*1 Samuel 1:9–2:2 &19*

More than anything else in the whole world, Hannah wanted a son. Every day she dreamed of holding her own baby boy, of cuddling him and singing to him; but it was just a dream. Years came and years went, and still, Hannah had no son. But even in her darkest days, hope was living in Hannah's heart. God had planted it there. Hannah held on to hope. And Hannah kept praying.

"Please, God, please," cried Hannah in the temple. "Would you give me a baby boy? If you will answer my prayer, I promise to give my son back to you. I will bring him here, to the temple, and he will be your servant."

And what do you think happened? One day, Hannah had her own baby boy! Hannah held little Samuel; she cuddled him and sang to him, just like she had dreamed. And when Samuel was old enough, Hannah took him to live in the temple, just as she had promised.

As Hannah blew her son a kiss goodbye and set off for home, she began to sing a song of praise to God, who had heard her prayers and kept hope alive in her heart.

**God's Wonderful Words to You**

I will give you hope.
Jeremiah 29:11

*This is my song of praise to you, for you have heard my prayer.*
*You whispered hope into my heart and kept it growing there.*
*You make me strong; you make me glad, and every day I'll sing.*
*To thank you for the peace and love and all the hope you bring!*

Dear _____,

Did you know that hope can live in the darkest of places? Think about the deep soil where daffodil bulbs are hidden. One day, pretty flowers will emerge from the dark earth. Or think about a chrysalis, hanging from a branch, all shriveled and lifeless. But inside, a butterfly is growing. One day, she will spread her wings and fly. Now think about Hannah. Even in her darkest days, hope was alive in her heart. And just like I whispered hope into Hannah's heart, I will whisper hope into your heart too. Even in the darkest times, keep praying. Hold on to hope. It is my gift to you.

With Love,
GOD

As soon as Hannah got home, she took out her needles and thread and began to make a special coat for Samuel. It was just the first of many. Every year, Hannah would take a beautiful homemade coat to her son, and every single stitch would be sewn in love.

# The Servant Girl

*2 Kings 5:1–15*

Sometimes, when the stars shone bright and all was quiet, Naaman's servant girl would close her eyes as she lay on her little mat and dream of the home she had left behind. She missed Israel. She missed her family. But even though she had been carried far away to this strange land to become a servant, she did not lose her faith in God; she did not feel sorry for herself. Instead, she felt sorry for her master, Naaman.

Naaman had a horrible skin disease. And even though he had a very important job in the army, and even though he was very rich, his power and money could not help. No medicine or cream could cure his leprosy. No doctor had ever been able to take that horrible skin disease away. But the little servant girl knew someone who *could*. And one day, she spoke to her mistress.

"Mistress," the little servant girl said. "If only my master would travel to Israel and ask to see Elisha. Elisha knows God. I'm sure that with God's help, he will be able to heal my master."

And so Naaman set out for Israel. It seemed as if he was gone for many days and many nights. Every morning the little servant girl would do her chores—make the beds, clean the house—but all the time she wondered, would her master be cured? Would God take his leprosy away?

Finally, the day came when Naaman returned home. As he jumped down from his horse, the little servant girl saw that his skin was perfect! All the leprosy had disappeared. Naaman's servant girl giggled with delight as she heard the story of how Elisha had told her master to dip seven times in the River Jordan; and when he came out, he was healed!

But her favorite part of the story was hearing how Naaman had shouted, "Now I know there is no God in all the world except in Israel!"

The little servant girl had known that all along. And now, Naaman knew it too.

Dear _____,

Don't you think it's wonderful how that little girl kept her faith in me and shared it with others? I bet no one in Naaman's house thought a servant girl was important, but she became priceless to Naaman! And here's a little secret: it doesn't matter whether your job is to clean houses or command an army— the important thing is to keep your faith in me and share it with others. And you will be priceless to me.

Love,
GOD

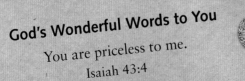

**God's Wonderful Words to You**

You are priceless to me.
Isaiah 43:4

# Esther

# The Prayerful Girl

*Esther 2–8*

Esther trembled as she looked at her reflection in the mirror. Her silver crown sparkled in the sunlight. The golden beads in her dress danced like diamonds. Here she was, sitting in the royal palace, the wife of King Xerxes, the queen of Persia. But inside her heart, she was still that young, frightened Jewish girl with a big decision to make.

Haman, the king's wicked advisor, had somehow managed to convince her husband that all the Jews should be killed. Esther had a choice. She could keep quiet and hope King Xerxes would not find out she was a Jew herself; or she could be brave and try to save the lives of all her people. It was a rule in the palace that no one was allowed to talk to the king unless he invited them to do so. If Esther approached his royal throne uninvited, she might be killed! But in her heart, Esther already knew what she had to do.

Esther wrote a note and gave it to her handmaid. "Take this letter to my cousin, Mordecai, who is waiting for my decision. I will go to the king. But first, Mordecai must gather all our people together. They must eat nothing for three days, and they must pray, pray, pray. Tell him I will be doing the same."

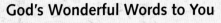

**God's Wonderful Words to You**
Call out to me when trouble comes.
I will save you.
Psalm 50:15

Her handmaid hurried out, and Esther sank to her knees and prayed to God for help.

Three days later, Esther put on her royal robes, and trembling in fear, she approached King Xerxes' throne. Would he permit her to speak? What would happen when he found out she was a Jew? But Esther need not have worried. God had heard her prayers. The king smiled as his beautiful bride approached. "What is it, my queen?" he asked her. "Anything I have is yours."

"My king," Esther whispered. "If you love me, please save my life, and the lives of all my people." King Xerxes sprang to his feet in shock when he discovered how Haman had plotted to kill all the Jews, including his beautiful wife. "My dear," he said, as he took Esther's trembling hand in his. "Don't worry. I will spare your life and the lives of all your people." Esther cried tears of joy. And the streets and alleyways outside the palace were filled with the sounds of praise and rejoicing for Queen Esther, who bravely saved her people. But Esther knew she had not really saved them. God had.

Dear _____,

I am so glad Queen Esther called out to me when she was worried. She knew that I was the only one who could save her and her people. What do you do when trouble comes your way?

I hope you remember to call out to me. Pray, pray, pray, like Queen Esther did. I am always there, right by your side, ready to listen, ready to bring you hope.

Your Friend,
GOD

# The Young Girl

*Luke 1:28–38; 2:1–20*

In the stillness of a Bethlehem night, a lullaby rang out soft and clear under the starlit sky. In the darkness, a young girl was singing to her newborn baby. The girl was Mary, and her son was Jesus.

In the little stable, Joseph was sleeping. The donkey, the cows, and the sheep were all sleeping too. But Mary was wide awake, holding her tiny treasure in her arms and thinking about everything that had happened.

She would never forget that night, just nine months ago, when an angel told her she had been chosen to be the mother of God's Son. She remembered how afraid she was and how she didn't understand what it meant. And now here she was, holding her little boy.

**God's Wonderful Words to You**

You are in my hand.
Jeremiah 18:6

Mary watched Jesus as he slept. He looked just like any other ordinary baby. Mary smiled at his chubby fingers curled around hers and his little eyelashes softly closed against his cheeks. But in her heart, Mary knew that Jesus was not ordinary. How could he be, when those shepherds had burst into the stable not long ago, because angels from heaven had told them a special baby had been born?

What did it mean when they knelt at her baby's feet? Even their sheep seemed to gaze at him in wonder! "Here's our Savior," the shepherds had whispered in awe. But how could this tiny child be a savior? Mary wondered what would happen to her baby when he grew up. She had so many questions. And she was still afraid. But as she rocked her sleeping son in her arms, peace wrapped itself around her like a big, warm blanket. And in the darkness, Mary knew that just like she was holding Jesus, she was being held in God's huge, strong hand.

Mary laid her baby in the manger, closed her eyes, and fell asleep. She was in God's hand, and nothing else mattered.

Dear _____,

Do you ever have questions that you can't find the answers to? Mary had so many questions, but as soon as she realized I was holding her, all her fears went away. Did you know that I am holding you too? When you lie down to go to sleep, you are in my hand. When you wake up in the morning, you are in my hand. When you feel afraid, lonely, or sad, you are in my hand. No matter what you do or how you feel, you will always be safe in my strong hand.

Love,

GOD

# The Thirsty Girl

*John 4:4–28*

The Samaritan woman sank down by the well in the heat of the noonday sun. She was tired, thirsty, and unhappy. Her troubles felt as heavy as the water jar on her shoulder. She dropped it in the sand where it fell with a loud thud. Was there no rest for her? How could it be that with all her searching she could not seem to find love? Why did her heart feel so dry inside, like a big, thirsty hole that needed to be filled?

"Could you get me a drink?" a voice called out.

The Samaritan woman was so wrapped up in her own thoughts she did not see Jesus sitting by the well. She was shocked. Why was he talking to her?

"Sir," she replied, "you are not from my town. Why are you asking me for water? You don't know me."

"But I *do* know you," said Jesus. "I know everything about you. I know you are unhappy and have been searching for love." The Samaritan woman looked at Jesus. How could he know such things? Who was this man who had love in his eyes and peace in his words?

"Look at this water," Jesus said softly. "One day, this well will dry up and all the water will be gone. But did you know the love God has for you will never run dry? It's a love that will last forever. God is the one who can fill your heart with love, hope, rest, and peace."

The woman sprang to her feet. Suddenly, she did not feel tired anymore. She felt as if Jesus had lifted that heavy load from her heart. She laughed, and with a lightness in her step, she ran back into town, shouting to all who would listen, "Come, come! Meet the man who knows me and knows you!" And by the well, where Jesus sat, the Samaritan woman left her heavy water jar and all her unhappiness behind.

### God's Wonderful Words to You

Come to me, all you who are tired and are carrying heavy loads. I will give you rest.
Matthew 11:28

Dear _____,

Have you ever carried a big, heavy backpack that you couldn't wait to put down? That's how the Samaritan woman felt when she went to the well. She was so weighted down with worry and unhappiness. But when she met Jesus, it was as if he took her heavy load away. Jesus can do the same for you too. Come to him, whenever you are tired, whenever you have worries. He will take all that away, and he will give you love, hope, rest, and peace.

Love,
## GOD

# The Forgiven Girl

*John 8:1–11*

The woman could not escape. Two men held her arms tightly as they pushed her in front of Jesus. "Jesus!" the teachers of the law shouted. "Look at this woman. We caught her sinning. Our law says she should be stoned. What do *you* think?"

Jesus looked up at the angry men. Each one held a large stone in his hand. The woman was looking down, crying. Her tears fell quietly onto the dusty floor where they made small pools of sadness. Jesus knelt down and began to write in the sand with his finger, and everyone waited to see what would happen. What was he writing? No one knew.

Jesus stood up. He wasn't thinking about the law these men followed. He was thinking about Eve, the first woman who God made, and how God had covered her with love and forgiveness.

"Is there anyone here who has never done anything wrong? If there is, he can throw the first stone."

Everything was quiet. The men all looked at each other. Then they looked down. The oldest scratched his beard. He had done something wrong that very morning. He could not throw his stone. He dropped it on the ground. And one by one, every man did the same. The woman heard the quiet *thud, thud, thud* behind her as every single stone fell to the sand. And when she lifted her eyes, only Jesus was there. "Go home," Jesus said softly. "And make good choices."

The woman's tears of sadness turned into tears of joy. Jesus had set her free! She left, just like Eve, all wrapped up in God's love and forgiveness. And as she ran home, she knew that Jesus must have written a new law in the sand. It was the law of love.

Dear _____,

Can you guess what the law of love says? It says: forgive others; be gentle with them; respect all people; be kind; treat others as you would want them to treat you. And if you need someone to show you how to do these things, just look at Jesus! Jesus came to teach us how to love and forgive—just like he loved and forgave that woman. If you can follow the law of love it will free you from hate, from not being able to forgive, and from judging others. Follow the law of love—because it's the only law that really will set you free.

Love,
GOD

**God's Wonderful Words to You**

I will set you free.
Isaiah 44:22

23

# The Busy Girl

*Luke 10:38–41*

There was not a moment to waste. Martha quickly straightened the curtains as she peered through the window down the street. Any minute now, Jesus would arrive with his disciples. Martha had been busy all day. She had swept every step, cleaned every cupboard, and dusted every doorknob. What else did she need to do?

Martha quickly checked her long to-do list. Had she forgotten anything? Roll the bread, check; wash the grapes, check; dust the furniture, check; set the table, check. Wait! She still needed to make sure the fire was hot enough to bake the little bread rolls she made earlier that morning. Martha scurried to the kitchen, quickly flung her apron over her head, and got to work.

A few moments later, Jesus arrived. Martha hurriedly put the bread to bake and ran to greet him at the door. "Jesus, Jesus!" she cried, as she hugged him. "We're so glad you're here. Take a seat. I've made a delicious meal and it's almost ready."

Martha ran back to the kitchen, lifted the bread from the fire, and arranged it neatly on a plate. She cleaned the cups, poured the water, filled the dishes with fruit, and began to carry everything to the table. Wait! There were not enough cushions for everyone to sit on as they ate. She would have to run to the neighbor's house to borrow some, and she still needed to polish the plates! It was all *too* much. How could she do everything all by herself? And where was her sister, Mary, when she needed her the most? And then Martha saw Mary, sitting quietly at Jesus' feet, doing nothing. How lazy! Martha marched into the living room. "Jesus!" she cried. "I'm so busy getting everything ready. Please tell my sister to help me."

Jesus smiled. "Martha, Martha," he said kindly. "You are worried about many things. But Mary is not being lazy. She is listening to me, and that is always a good choice."

For the first time that day, Martha stopped. She thought about what Jesus said. Maybe, just maybe, Jesus was right. Perhaps being busy was not always best.

Dear _____,

Do you ever feel like you have too much to do? Maybe you feel like Martha sometimes—so busy with chores, schoolwork, and sports activities. But if you fill your day with rushing around and being busy, there'll be no room to listen to Jesus! At some point in your day, stop. Be still. Listen to Jesus. Is time with him on your to-do list? Try to put that at the top. Time with Jesus is *always* a good choice.

Love,

GOD

**God's Wonderful Words to You**

Be still, and know that I am God.
Psalm 46:10

25

# The Generous Girl

*Luke 21:1–4*

In her little room, the poor widow shook her bank to see how much money she had saved. Two tiny copper coins fell into the palm of her hand. The widow sighed. Should she give it all to the church? Yes—it was not much, but it was all she had. She put the two small coins in her pocket and set off.

In his big palace, the rich man picked up his treasure box to see how much money he had saved. Wow! It was so heavy! All the gold coins sparkled as he peeked inside. The rich man smiled. Should he give it all to the church? No—half would be enough. Then he would still have half left for himself. He put the gold coins in his pocket and set off.

At the temple, the rich man was first in line. He proudly stomped up to the offering box and threw his gold coins in, one at a time. The heavy coins clinked loudly as they bounced in the box. Good! The rich man hoped that everyone was watching. Then they would all know how rich he was.

Next in line was the poor widow. She quietly tiptoed up to the offering box, took the two tiny copper coins out of her pocket, and slipped them in. The two little pennies dropped with hardly a sound. Good! The poor widow hoped that nobody was watching. Then no one would know how poor she was.

But someone *was* watching. Someone was sitting in the corner. He had seen the rich man. He had seen the poor widow. Jesus had seen everything. "Who do you think gave the most?" Jesus asked his disciples. "Was it the rich man, or the poor widow?"

"Oh, the rich man, of course," the disciples replied. But Jesus shook his head.

"No," he said quietly. "That poor widow gave far, far more than the rich man, because she gave everything she had. She might not have lots of money, but she has lots and lots of love." And Jesus smiled, because to be rich in love is the most wonderful thing in the world.

Dear _____,

Did you know that when you are kind, you share, or when you are generous, you are living a life of love? And it's so much better to have lots and lots of love rather than lots of money—because you can never lose love, and no one can *ever* take it away.

Love,

GOD

**God's Wonderful Words to You**

Lead a life of love.
Ephesians 5:2

27

# The Grateful Girl

*John 12:1–8; Matthew 26:10–13*

Mary of Bethany was worried. She knew something terrible was going to happen to Jesus. Everyone in Jerusalem knew it. You only had to shop in the marketplace or walk in the streets to hear the whispers and lies people were telling about him. Jesus had enemies. And one day soon, Mary knew that Jesus would die.

What could she do? What could Mary give to Jesus to show how much she loved him? And then, Mary saw it. The big, beautiful alabaster jar that was full of expensive perfume. She would give that to Jesus!

Mary peeked through the open door where Jesus sat at the table having dinner with his disciples. Carefully, she carried the jar and crept quietly into the room. Without a sound, she knelt on the floor and poured the perfume over Jesus' feet. A wonderful scent rose in the air. It traveled over the table, curled around the curtains, and filled the room like a whisper of love.

"What are you doing?" the men around the table cried. "That is expensive perfume! What a waste!"

But Jesus smiled at Mary as she dried his feet with her hair. "Leave her alone," Jesus said softly. "Mary has done a beautiful thing for me. What she has done today will always be remembered."

In that moment, Mary's worries disappeared. Her heart filled with a peace she had never known before. And even though the scent of the perfume would soon be gone, the peace Jesus brought to her heart would last forever.

Mary had poured out her perfume. Jesus had poured out his peace.

Dear _____,

Did you know that *you* can do beautiful things for Jesus too? Every prayer you whisper, every kind word you say, every minute you spend helping others—these are all beautiful things that you can do for Jesus, and not one of them is ever wasted. Do beautiful things for Jesus, and let him give you his peace.

Love,
GOD

**God's Wonderful Words to You**

I leave my peace with you.
John 14:27

# The Happy Girl

*John 20*

Mary Magdalene thought her heart might burst with joy as she ran through the streets of Jerusalem. It was early in the morning, but the whole world was awake—every bird singing high in the treetops and every flower dancing in the wind seemed to know this was no ordinary day.

The disciples would never believe what just happened. Mary could hardly believe it herself. Could it *really* be true that she had just been talking to Jesus? Everyone knew he died on the cross three days earlier. Everyone knew his body had been carried away to that quiet cave on the hillside. But only Mary knew the cave was now empty. Jesus was alive! He had spoken to her! And when he called her name, and reached out his arms in love, Mary's fears flew away. Jesus was alive, and his perfect, precious love was all she needed.

Mary picked up her skirt and ran without stopping until she reached the little house where the disciples were hiding in the room upstairs. She took the stairs two at a time and burst through the door. Out of breath, her eyes shining with tears, Mary shouted out her unbelievable news, "I have seen the Lord!"

They were the greatest words the world would ever hear. The cave was empty. But Mary's heart was full.

**God's Wonderful Words to You**

Perfect love drives away fear.
1 John 4:18

Dear _____,

Can you imagine how Mary felt that morning?
Only three days earlier, the unthinkable happened.
Jesus had died! Mary's heart had been full of fear.
But on that glorious morning, Jesus filled her heart
with his perfect, precious love.

He wants to fill *your* heart too. Jesus is reaching out
to you. Hear him calling your name. You are his
precious daughter. Put your hand in his. Let Jesus
take you in his arms. He will hold you with his
perfect love and never, ever let you go.

I Love You,
GOD

UPDATED EDITION

# My Love Letter to God

If you could write a letter
And put it in God's hand
You know that God would read it,
And truly understand—
Everything you're feeling,
Every word you'd say,
You're God's precious daughter—
Write to God today...